I am
BARBARA

BARBARA BELLINGER

I AM BARBARA

iUniverse books may be ordered through booksellers or by contacting:

iUniverse
1663 Liberty Drive
Bloomington, IN 47403
www.iuniverse.com
1-800-Authors (1-800-288-4677)

ISBN: 978-1-5320-7238-3 (sc)
ISBN: 978-1-5320-7237-6 (e)

Print information available on the last page.

iUniverse rev. date: 03/28/2019

To my Readers

The words in this book are words of Praise, I Praise my Family

For all the love and support that they have given me throughout the years

To my friends that I call brothers and sisters in Christ I am so happy
to with you on this Christian journey.... I dedicate this book to all of you
for being part of Duck's story

I Am Barbara

Getting off exit 98 from off of HWY 95, south…

I am returning home to the country of my birth,

In these United States of America, it's called South Carolina.. Turning on to exit 98, it's as if I went back in time, as if time stood still here, as I merge into the town, I do see something's a new, a traffic light and Band name Motels mmm, the strip has really grown up. The entire amenity for a weary traveler could need when a rest area won't do. But yet, there's cleanliness about it, the kind you can walk with your shoes off, and not be worried about broken glass. The Blue sky, the bellowed clouds that move so slowly and change into shapes, haha there's one shaped like a hand pointing its finger, pointing me to the way home, straight ahead.

As the song says, the long and winding road that leads to your door, you left me waiting here such a long, long time ago. Don't leave me waiting here lead me to your door. As the road drives me back in time, I could still call the names of to whom these houses be long, but I guess now it would be their grandchildren, or even great-grands. How proud the spirits of the old ones must be, to see the wooden shacks transform into fine brick houses and well kept lawns and shapely hedges...Gone are the days of sweeping the yard with Shaw brooms and the horses and cows eating the grass to keep it groomed, as I recall my grandparents yard was made of sand. Just go to prove that climate change is real, due to all the storms and floods that has pass through here, the earth beneath our feet has changed, from sand to solid black dirt and luscious green grass .The sun flicker through the tall pine trees that line the old HWY six the flood of memories of faces and moments in time, that's long since gone from sight, but the old school days, songs playing on the radio makes this experience beautiful like a warn bubble bath and a cold glass of wine. Just up ahead the steeple to the family church, AAAAH there she is, still standing strong, and stately. There she is, just like I've always known her to be, the spring that flows through all these fields that keeps life growing here in this Village and all the graves there holes the history of the blood sweat and tears that made this wonderful place, just what it is a wonderful place.

My grandfather Man-Bryant started this grave yard off to be the family orientated order that its in..He would make sure that all family member where buried in the same area, the old saying was, where ever man-Bryant say you be placed, that's where you go and still yet today his grandsons are the care takers of this hallowed ground. This entire place is Hallowed ground to me, I've walked, run, fall, and played the whole three hundred acres of this land of young's road. It is so amazing to me how my life has come full circle. How I've landed back to the place of my birth and back into the arms of the man that loved me even through time we didn't even know if we were still alive somewhere in this great big old world.

And here it is, almost thirty years later, a brand new start, alright Barbara it's time to live FOR YOUR LEGACY...those that where in that small board house in the front room sitting around Man and Bell's potbelly stove the night of my birth, has long gone on to be with the Lord.

As I stand here on this plot of land that my dear mother made sure of...Yes reading the deed and title reads like a document of descendant ship, from my mother, form her mother,from her father....yes written in black and white, I'm supposed to be here.

When I was born here, I arrived with nothing and I returned with nothing either.

No none of the baggage I accumulated along the way back here, I am free, yes free of all the bullshit. My head is clear of what I want for the part of the rest of my life that God has granted me. Free to love in truth, to trust without fear, to feel hurt without regret. Yes to love God the Father in the way He gives me understanding of what he gave me this life for in the first place.

I no longer say that my addiction is in the parking lot doing pushups, waiting for me to kill my ass …No I sit on my porch with a good cup of coffee and listen to the brides sing and feel the breeze on my face and say Lord how may I serve you today. And off into the world of this little village I go. Just the walk across the yard to my car is praise, the grass beneath my once was a field that my grandparents planted peas. The drive way is the same one, which the old wagon hauled cotton in and out of. Yes the patch of dirt that I call a driveway was made by wagon wheels and the pressing of many feet that were blessed on their going out and coming in. During my time in jail and rehab stays, I often dreamt about this highway, and when it came to the fork in the road. That's where I'd lose my bearings; the dream would always venture off to a dirt road or a highway I was trying to get back to where ever it was I came from. So you could imagine how awe struck I was when they built an exit highway to make it easy to get to HWY 95, north or South. It was like driving in a dajahvo, there are a lot of things that a peaceful mind will make you question about reality, and yes you sometimes have to pinch yourself to make sure you're not dreaming. The town has the same old buildings that were once the hub of the life and livelihood of this village. The trips to town in the wagon I can still feel the giggling and shaking, the humps and bumps of the ride. I can even hear the warnings of what not to do or ask for once we got there, so her, now I'm driving in my car into the parking lot of a change store. Something my grandparents didn't live to see. That good looking bank and the fine gas stations, all on these smooth pave roads. The old pathways are now sidewalks, the lovely park in the heart of town; commemorate those that put this town on the map by selling bricks with an ancestor name on it, to be placed on the walkway of the entrance of the park. Yes you can go there and find the names of the old ones. Yes their names are there, Binna, William, Man Bryant&Maybelle, Hop Joe, and Umi & Rock. Yes there is a brick with those names on it.

Now to the real purpose for me writing this book, I just want to keep my promise that I'll never go back. The word repents means to turn away from, and I have, I've turned away FROM ALL THE THINGS that separated me from all the ones I love and loves me. The Bible says look I make all things new, and yes He has.

Everything is new, it's the same as when they pulled our mobile home on the land and they handed me the key, when I opened that door and walked in and the smell of the new carpet the fresh paint, the clean walls the echo of my voice, the click of the light switch, the flush of the toilet, the turning on of the water in the sink. All was new and even though I have called many a places home, places where I lived. None was like this; this is home, where my mind is clear, clear enough to set a plan in place.

Seeing the big picture, seeing Barbara.........................

So keeping my promise to myself that should I make it this far, I would leave something of myself for my decedents to come and to thank everyone that I love and that love me along the way, this book will be the testament of this wonderful life.

In this book I will share with you photos and poems I've written and I pray they will entertain you and just melt your heart. I can only write from my view point of my life and recollections of the pass, I can't say how anyone feels about a moment in time or how one may see things in a different light. All I know is I love I, love everyone that I mention in this book, and I just thought it would be nice for my decedents to know of you too. After all we are living in a world at this time, of instant gratification we are quickly to forget to say Love you, thank you, forgive me, and excuse me. Our surrounding change so quickly you forget what was or even where it was.

When I returned home for good good, this was after my mom died and I had to go back to New York for almost a year. My book obedience is Better than Sacrifice was just published and we had to move out the house my mother and I shared, and the land she left me wasn't quite ready for me to move on it, and Michael had just started a business venture with a close friend of his.

I was not in the state of mind to be homeless or live with my cousin, so I went to New York stayed with my daughter got my own apartment it was dead winter and I tell you. It was the most beautiful New York moment in my life. I had my children and a car, the car made all the difference. I was able to go place with my family and go to where I needed to be to sell my books and make speeches back tracking to the places that helped me along the way, it was awesome going back and letting them see all the work paid off, sharing my story in the presence of the ones who help made it possible. The joy I had when I knocked on the door of my parole officer Mr. Furman it was joy and sorrow at the same time. He was gravely ill, I'm happy I got to tell him Thank You, for believing in me and yes I got the guy I thought got away(Michael) and I plan to go back to Eutawville and spend the rest of my life with him. New York didn't let me get away that easy, with everything my apartment was on the fourth floor. Boy oh boy, I tell you I didn't come back home till I was done with whatever I was out and about doing. When I was lucky enough to get a parking space next to the building, I stayed in, till a whole day was planned out with me and my daughter and the kids. Yes I got to go through those doors that I left partly open and shut them real tight behind me. I went to Harlem and stood in front of Rev. McFadden's building and yelled up at the window (Mac) and listen to my voice fad away in the air and I was satisfied that he wasn't there and just like in my recurrent dreams I got disorientated when finding the street that John Merlin use to live on and I stood outside the building that I thought might have been the one he lived in and I sat on the stoop and just breath. And there it was my answer, yes all has changed just keep it moving Barbara nothing to see here. But then the sprit showed me a sign, I ran into someone I knew and boy was he glad to see me. We laugh and remotest and at the very end he asked if I had a couple of dollars I could throw a brother. I look into his eyes and I saw the demons of that life that I came here to close the door tight on and I said to those demons, no I got nothing for you got in my car and didn't even look in my rear view mirror when I drove off. What I did do was go to my daughter's house and told her to get her and the kids ready to take a trip to Eutawville. Yes it was time to go and see if things were ok with my man and my land.

But would you know it!! A snow strong canceled that trip; to me it was another sign from the sprit. I went and brought me a shovel and I dug my car out of the snow and I did a hallelujah dance in the middle of the street, yes heavenly Father I am strong enough to dig my way out. We got to Eutawville and it was warm like spring time and my man looked like a tall glass of sweet tea.

The best part about this trip was that the plans we made are working out, we went and put a down payment on our mobile home, but the land just wasn't ready yet, but Michael was handling his business and putting the pressure on the folks about the land. That's one thing about Michael he is one who gets things done, if he can't do it he knows someone who can.

Yes I missed my man some kind of awful,

I slept well that night, so my man asked me to come on back to Eutawville and I had to tell him the truth. I am not running from anything I'm running towards what will have to be for the rest of my life on this earth, that's our love being lived in our home on the land, my mama left it to me, to come back before that is put in place that would mean I'd have to stay with you at Skeet's house, and I don't want to be in that kind of atmosphere. So I went back to New York, I wasn't back a week when Michael called and told me the land was clear and we could move on it, That's all I needed to hear, I donated everything in my apartment and whatever my nephew Corell couldn't fit in my van I left it there. The sprit showing me something again, when I first left New York same thing, happened, I said yes Lord I know how to let go and what I leave behind let it be a blessing to someone else. After dropping my nephew of, I went to say goodbye to my daughter, and my grand-children, I knew it would be a while before I'd see them again, my daughter and I had the long talk I needed, the one that made me think while on the trip back home just how blessed we are. You see now that's the thing about my daughter, that makes so glad she's my child, the words of wisdom that come out her mouth, she's the one that should write a book, uh I tell you. She spoils me every time we are together and she keeps me in her circle of need to know bases only. Through my daughter I have three other daughters, so that makes me have a slew full of grandchildren. Yes my short but wonderful, stay in New York this time was well spent. I stopped in Baltimore to see my son, I tell you, I am one proud, and for all the things my son has overcome and made it out of them streets. He had nothing to do with raising him. I mean look like him, talk like him, love the red, black, and green flag just like his father. I sat down and had the talk with my son to let him know and to understand that there's a man in my life and he is in it to stay. And that I love him very much and I want you to respect that and when you come to Eutawville to see your mother the home you enter in will be his and mine, I had to have this talk with my son, because he has never seen me in such a made up mind when it came to a man in my life, my son has always known that a man is in my life for a reason and being in love wasn't one of them, my son says so long as your happy Umi, time will tell. I saw my son graduate earning his Master of Science; it hangs on my wall in my office

When I finally got on the highway heading back to Eutawville, I had a lot to think about. Everyone said what was on their minds about how much I have changed and they are so happy for me. I look in my rear view marrow and then the side one and the one that let you see where you're going I put my book of roses CD in the CD player and the highway was smooth sailing.

EUTAWVILLE HERE I COME.........................

HERE ARE A FEW PHOTOS FUN WITH MY
FAMILY IN MY NEW YORK APARTMENT,

the last time I got to be with my sister Gwen and my sister Ellen. The next time new was together we were holding her hand on her death bed. I was so happy my Brother Wayne got to see her too. We all got to tell Gwen how much we love her. But we chose to remember Gwen when she was at her best. The day at her sons Corel's wedding, we had a wonderful time and we all looked good, we were truly a family that day. I was living in South Carolina then matter of fact I just moved down there.

And on this trip for Corel's wedding I made the decision, to take my mother back with me, everybody gave her the ok and she said, fine if yall think that's best, and so it was.

I was so happy in my sprit, that now I have the opportunity, to care for my mother and give her back the love that he so,so deserve from me. I was eager to make her life as comfortable as possible and give her her heart desire.

THE JOY OF BEING WITH MY GRANDCHILDREN

Lizzy and Breah and Isaiah

THIS BLUE VAN MADE NEW YORK SO MUCH
EASIER, than buses and trains.

Breah and Umi our Love

She never let lose sight of Better Days

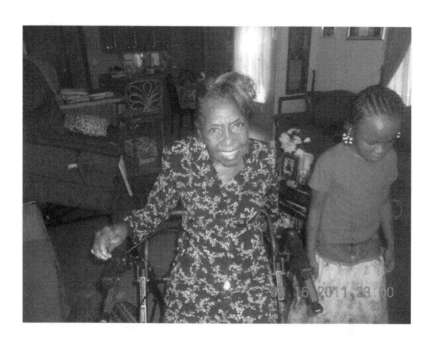

Hop and Felicia in our home in South Carolina

Elaine and Felicia my brother's two daughters, they stayed with mommy and I for a year and we had a good time, Breah sent them a dance game for Christmas mommy and I got a kick out of them master the game, before you knew it they knew all the dances on that game

Yes it was time now to get settled on the land my
mother left me, the same land her mama lift her.

Michael and I still had to stay at Skeets house just a little bit longer, but with the Grace of God this too shall past.

I even got a job and I got the chance to meet Charlie Davis, the man that trained the horse Secretary.

Then we move out from skeet and we got a job a hotel and we lived there for a while.

Then the sprit came to show me something again. The experience from working that business taught me about cash flow and how to manage it yes, the sprit was showing me something and believe you me, I was in my Bible and in my prayer closet getting myself ready for the war that was coming. The mobile home we picked out wasn't ready to be pulled on the land, because all the things I asked to be change or to be touched up hadn't been finish yet, so we went back to Skeets house.

And when we got back there, I understood what the sprit was telling me to be prepared for, People she trusted was tiring to take her house.

The Lord moved me to take on these people and get Skeet out this mess. We went to court and Skeet won her case, but unfortunately she died before she could enjoy the fruits of her labor. I still yet today when I drive pass her house I say thank you Skeet.. Even though you may be doing Skeet a good thing by being there to help her out for letting you stay in her house, things got done. Food was bought, cloths where washed

The house was kept clean; the wilding out was cut to a minimal. I can say this she gave me the Best house gift, her mother's China Cabinet. I turned it into a shrine to my mother and loved ones that has passed.

Yes home sweet home, I put the letters R & B, on the house that stands for Rock and Barbara. They were made just for us a young lady that works at the bank made them for us.

Figure 1 with scenery like this finding your way
back home is something you want to do

This tree was planted by my mom, we had to cut it down and grind the roots to make sure it didn't grow back, because we had to put the back of the mobile home where it was. So we cut the tree into logs and I lined the driveway with them. The tree trunk I left alone I save it and it's on the back of the house standing tall with the evidence the strong branches were on her. The sprit spoke to me about that, the tree is like my mother, tall and strong with big thick roots, her children like the branches are cut off gone their own separate ways,she had to be up rooted from this good ground, so the next genartion can take root here, in this good ground where roots run deep and everything that is planted here will grow.

The tree my mother planted, that I had to cut down.

What makes my story such a success is the family support I have. Whenever I need to watch a sermon, I can look at any of my aunts and uncles and cousins lives and take away from their example and know where my moral compass needle should be pointing towards. My uncle Big Boy always says If Bell Bryant chilen can't do it, it can't be done, why? Because we have a touch of class. And there aren't no ugly people in our family, if we bring'em in ugly they stick with us we'll make'um look good. I remember one time at a family get together this was right after I gave my life back to Christ; I pulled my uncle Big Boy to the side and asked him, Rev. Bryant how do I know that I am living a Christ like life. He answered me with this, and I quote whenever anyone can walk up on you and find you doing the right thing. From then on I always judge others as I judge myself, what all I've been through to get to this point please thank God that it wasn't you.

I am awake to the fact that I can thank God it wasn't me, oh my goodness the stories I know now of people I care about, that has overcome. Hallelujah we made it out. My uncle Big Boy has many saying and in his sermons the messages are always about overcoming, in the back of my Bible I have written down at least ten of his sermons.

When I look back, uncle Big Boy was always there in times of moral support.

Especially the day my father was murdered, he was the one that came and told me in the gentlest manner that could ever be handled that way. He came to my house and when the voice over the intercom said uncle Big Boy, I knew this wasn't just a casual visit. There had to be something wrong, he tapped on the door ever so lightly, I guess knowing that I'd be at the door. When I opened it he put his hands on both my shoulders and said Duck your mama needs you. In every situation and circumstance you remember his powerful prayers. After he prays you can handle whatever comes next, because you know God is in control. I even got him on my YouTube channel talking about why he so smart. Now being alive for eighty plus I do think you should have some smarts about you. Now I enjoy the weekly visits and trips with him to the V.A. and accompanying him to the many church events that he is a part of. I sit in the audience and I am just busting with pride.

The only messed up thing about being a recovering addict, well for me anyway, total recall!!! I don't have it and it is a bummer. People I went to school with be like Barbara you mean you don't remember me I am like well tell who you are and let's get to know one another. And down here in the south people have total recall and they can get a bit upset with you when you don't recall it.

Don't let it have something to do with you being they girl or some kina feeling was involved oooh honey, they be tiring to make you remember, I be like we were six !!

I'm laughing as I write this, for real. No joke

My cousin Gene lives in the same area in the village for over sixty years he know everybody, I can tell him about I ran into so and so today and he tried to make me remember him and I'd say Gene you know who I'm talking about. Gene will tell me who they are, who they family is, tell you what that person about and how I know them and I would respond I was six!! That goes to show you why marriages down here in the village last 40, 50, 75 years. People even live to be 100 here. It is something and down here we believe in long engagements

I have cousins that have been engage for 15year, 20 year. All because of the family unit a family that pray together stays together and if health and where you live is at the top of the list as far as priority is concern we going to make sure family first.

But no you can't rule out, they just slow about.

I have one cousin, that truly don't have to worry about marriage or anything tiring him down I don't even think stays in a relationship but a minute, because by the time he tell them a pace of his mind telling them what he isn't goanna stand for, he's not bringing any ole thing to meet his mama. He is the whole package a mover and shaker gets things done and makes that choir sing, I say thank you Jason for always keeping it real with me and for not holding it against me for having told recall. I will always remember how you took care of you grandmother while she was in the hospital, I aint never saw nothing like that, When you get off the elevator all then nurses start scurrying around getting their clip board bring you up to date with her condition.

That's another thing about my cousin Jason he has accomplish a lot in his forty some odd years, they have this thing on the news that you send in the name of a teacher and they will come to the class and bring her or him a big thing of flowers and a gift card then show it on Tv that night..I've really been thinking about doing that for Jason.

He would get a kick out of it and then tell me. Don't you put me on blast like that no more?

That's Jason on the right with the family

as a family this is what we do, we support one another, on this night we were with our Uncle Rev. Willie Bryant.

We love family gatherings and at each other's homes. I love it when I ask the family to join us at our house, everybody shows up even, Mr. Bishop

The food is good and the joy is in the house.

We will sing songs, and move the table and make room on the floor to do the eclectic slid. The jokes be having us split our sides.

My first snow angel I made in my yard one for me and one for Rock.

We know how to have a good time

The thing Rev. Bryant wants us to always remember him for is that he always tried to keep the family together.

We Bryant girls love our uncle Decon William Bryant,
Tall brown and handsome.

Israel and Maybell Bryant

The one thing I can say about my family here in the village, they are disciplined and daily, weekly and monthly routines are a must and boy oh boy I tell you, you can set you watch by some of the things that we do every year. And I love it; you know church on Sunday and Bible study on Wednesday night. Then the traditions take up the rest of the year. I tell you the talent that is here in this village is awesome

That's why it so easy to come back come and settle in, The church we attend is a historical land mark..The Blood sweat and tear the old ones shed calling on Jesus to walk with them, heal their bodies, place their feet on higher ground and here we are. The ones the old one prayed for, and no I don't think WE have disappoint now when it comes to this next generation they a little punchy in the head. Back in the day, going to church was a must not a (I don't feel like it) ooooh you'd get something on you behind you'd still be thinking about it.

The hope and faith that the church gives you, you need it for your copping tools and having peace that stays with you.

On your job, at the barbershop, driving the school bus, dusting off all those items you have in your antique store.

Michael gives each one of the children in our church a dollar just for coming to Sunday school the Deacons have to ask the congregation every now and then to please bring their children to church. But third Sunday is children Sunday they wear their robes and sing their songs after that they are missing in action. I teach Sunday school every first and second Sunday. I love it so much, reading the story and watching them have a ah ah moment, when they understand what the bible lesson is about and what it has to do with their lives........

I love it when I bring my grandchildren on fifth Sunday and we think of a bible story and make a skit of the story. I dress them up in costumes and we have so much fun with it. And to the children that comes to Sunday school my sweet husband gives each one a dollar and they do look forward to it. We do what we can to encourage the children, that church and the Bible are something they need to know in their lives,

Mind and souls... and as they get older they will understand it better .

The fellowship of family and friends are so important in Michael and I lives, it's the fuel that keeps us going. Michael knew coming into our relationship how important being associated with a church would mean, just for the building blocks of a long and wonderful life.

He witness the joy I had in my personal relationship with my church family, partaking in many activities along with the women on the choir, doing praise dances and doing skits with his grandchildren on the fifth Sundays. Till one Sunday he got up and I said not yet honey, this is alter call. I thought he was getting up for prayer like we always do. He looked back at me and said I know Babe; he was getting up to join the church, the joy that filled my heart. I was so overcome that my cousins Kandy and Barbara had to come and comfort me. Yes, he went down in the water and he dived right into fellowship with the brothers of the church, he even joined the male chorus.

His children seen the change in their father and I tell you, the respect they have for our relationship is so much more than I could ever ask for. They call me by the endearing name Umi, just as my children do, so I don't too much miss out on grandmother duty so many things I'd love to do with mu children kids I get to do so much with Michael's grand's so I truly feel comfortable saying our children, our grandchildren.

What I do fine amazing, is how Michael and I lives were parallel to one another, when I left Eutawville in 1988 or 89 we were going through the same things and we kind of met in the flock in the road some 20 years later in 2009.I'd often think of him and he often thought of me when ever he'd pass through on HWY #6. So one night while driving home from a social church function. We pulled into the driveway of the little house where we first met and we prayed, Thanking God for the Love He reunited us with.

The Male chorus..to see Rock sing with the Brothers its Awesome, that's him being a part of a ministry....

Michael and I at our grand-daughter Destiny's christening, Dawayne and Vikkie's baby girl

Michael and I when we first met our grand-daughter
Yedjida, Isa and Intiah's baby girl

And just like me, even though we were out there in our mess. God took care of our children, what I mean by that, I'll say it again and again. We have the most wonderful, respectful, accomplished children that we could ever ask for, in other words our mess didn't mess with who they wanted to be as human being, and we thank God for that.

To watch them be the awesome parent, that they are is just plan wonderful. The quirky personalities my grandchildren have is so much fun, especially now day with all these technical stuff, I can video chat and it's just like being there, listening to the corny jokes and answering some of the darndest questions. One time our granddaughter Lizzy left me a message on the phone asking me, were in the world could I be this time of night? But if I'm on a date with pop-pop then alright, just call her later and tell her all about it. So you know I did. There's no way to change the pass, but when God gives you a second chance at being in your children's lives you'd best take it and be better than you shoulda,coulda,woulda been bull crap. Not money, not things, but time. Giving of your time to me that am the only thing that has the value of yourself that they can really hold on to, especially when we're dead and gone. Like when the time our son Isa was running a marathon in Atlanta Ga. Which was about a four hour drive, So I kept with Isa on the phone about when the event was going to be. Little did he know the Michael and I was going to drive there to see him in the race. When we got there I mean there were hundreds of people out there, how was I going to find our son amongst all these people, Michael said call him. So I did and the sprit showed me something again, the wonderful connection between mother and child. The echo on the phone when he answered, we just turned around and there we were right next to each other.

The joy was so loud. This is the photo the camera man took of us. Yes thats Isa with the red sleeve, yes God choose me to birth this beautiful man. He is father to Yedjida and Lover to Dr. Intiah and the culture that they have built around him and his family and friends is a wonderful aspect of life to have.Especailly now days. The black culture is so lost in this world of possessions, and the separations of the family unite. No fathers in the home, why because he's in jail. Children being raised by grandma, because mommy got to go back to school in order to get that job, which brings in that paycheck that would amount to if, she had her baby daddy bringing a paycheck together.

My son chooses to take a stand, not just for him. He's on a mission to have that village that raise a child in the real culture of true black man in a black nation, the one that's been here all the time. And every time I talk with him we always end with lets grow"

When the sprit showed me this connection that was what I needed from God, to let me know that I've made it to the next level of making amends. You see in recovery you have to seek forgiveness and make amends with everyone you can, you have to own your bull crap; so it don't own you. You can't go join the me to movement and not think of who you hurt just as bad, you need to explain yourself when necessary. You can't go around expecting everyone to forgive you for some of stunts you pulled trying to get money to feed your habit. Some people need to hear you say it. So they can heal from it too. Liked I said the total recall I don't have, and like I said maybe that's a good thing for me that is. I don't know about all people, you got to check yourself for that, but when someone brings it to your attention, you got to deal with it. Like one time I was in New York, visiting my our daughter Breah and we were having some laughs about back in the day and my daughter Kia told the story about the time I declared that I was grown and can handle smoking crack and how I'm Ms. Bee and I'm all that and a bag of chips..Oh child!! We

we had to laugh and hug it out with me. These three has been there for the good the bad the ugly of my addiction, but through it all they took care of me, God brought them together in a time in their lives when they need a family and they made one of their own. At their young ages they became care givers. Raised a family of their own, I'd need another book to tell that story. No matter how many came and went in and out of their lives they stayed together as sisters.No man or even location back against the wall situations didn't break their bond and they have beautiful grown men and women now that has given them grandchildren, then guess what!! God turned around and gave them more little babies, so they have lived two life times as mothers. You can call me selfish; it's ok because I believe God did that so I can live in what I missed the first time on seeing them be mommies......Hallelujah

In my home office my walls are cover with photos and memorabilia's of family and friends and things that I want to always remember that I hold near and dear to me. Like I keep reminding you, this total recall thing and me are not hand and hand.

This is why I do recommend that therapy is an essential part of recovery. Yes you may have family and church a good support system, for sure I do. But there are just some things you can't share with them you need therapy to give you clarity on some feeling or even dreams that you have as recurring often in your mind.

Things were so happy for me sometimes I had to stop and pray thanking God for the happiness, but then I got scared hoping that this wasn't a dream and that my reality was I was somewhere in a coma and this was all a coma dream, yes I sent my therapist through a loop with that one. I wasn't satisfied until she agreed to let me make up a pass word to say whenever I was having these feeling, just to reassure me this was real... I know!!! You may laugh, but you can get that happy and content with your life. Therapy is a tool to help you tighten up all those loose nuts and bolts in you changed life. With all this awareness you get from coming out of the fog, you need someone that's not so close to you. You need that someone to help you out thing in a proper perspective, because too, you can read things in the Bible and you swear the word is condemning you, but it's not. In Gods sweet redemption there is no condemnation, all is forgiven it is thrown into the sea of forgetfulness never to rise any more in the eye sight of God. Its man that bring stuff up and throw it in your face, oh if you are call to be a woman of God or man to preach the word of God. You going to have doubters because of your pass, even Jesus said a prophet is never received his own. Here's a kicker you may even have family members that look at your restored life and say time will tell. Then there are some that been so called stayed on the right track all they life, worked hard, been to school, retired from their job with a gold watch, and look at your restored life and feel you don't deserve it. And then there are those that are so happy for you that if you were to mess it all up and fall and don't even try to get back up it would just devastate them. I have a cousin Bernard, every time he comes home to Eutawville on his vacation he stops by our house and when he enters in the door he has a good laugh and a big hug for me, because he is so amazed at what the Lord has done in Michael and I lives. Bernard can tell my story because he knows all about my upbringing with my mom and dad. Bernard remembers me when I was the little girl that was so neat and tidy. He knew the story of who I am today all because of how God took all of my mistake and turned it all around for my good, He can't help but laugh with joy and say the words Duck I'm so proud of you. You want to know how you show your appreciation to the ones that prayed for you, put up with you nonsense, when you were going through. You show your repentance by never living that life again, and when you do fall short, you ask for help, you say I need someone to pray with me. Don't ever think you are alone. When your love ones see God pick you up and turn you around and place your feet on solid ground, you are not alone. They are so happy to be on this Christian journey with you.

When you insert yourself in a community that has the activities you need to alien yourself with, you get the benefit of hands on nurturing.

When I joined my first church in 2005 right after my baptism those sisters nurtured me.

They taught me how to talk, how to walk, how to dress. How to beautify myself not only on the outside but the inside. They showed me what to do with this love Jesus has for me. Then they fed me, they fed me the word of God. Oh it was bitter to the taste, but oh when it settled in my heart oh how sweet, sweeter than the honey on the honey cone. Yes just like fire shut up in my bones.. You hear the Ancient one say these words, but until you know it for yourself, the tears will flow and joy will be you're forever more. The importance of fellowship is your life line; you need this to see Gods love in other people. When you go around and see how other worship and give God the praise, be of service in the house of the Lord, the great reward you get when you help bring the church house into its full potential. When I sit back and hear the praises go up and someone says thank you Jesus or a Hallelujah is shouted deep from someone's soul. When you stand in the circle hand and hand and the prayer is be rendered you can't help but feel the Holy Spirit fall and you surrender to the will of God in your life....The Life that I've been giving to be here right now is the same as they say my second chance. From the time that I was born and then stolen from my parents then my children, BUT GOD!!! Oh yes God heard that prayer that somebody prated for me, had me on their mind and took the time and prayed for me. I'm so glad they prayed they prayed for me. Jesus paid the ransom and set me free and now I swore way up high with the spirit of God that lives within me, oh yes this new life that is free from the pass that use to hunt me in my dreams. No more sacrifices of myself just sweet obedience to the will of God on my life, and that's to have life more abundantly, not just give love but feel it not just have joy but be the joy, not want health and strength but have the mind and wear withal to know my body and mind to quite it down and breath, hear my heartbeat, feel the blood run through my veins.

Be the child of God which is sprit, be a sprit that is having a human experience.

For those of you, who like me are coming into your freedom the same as I have, go on learn new things, or relearn the things that you know you're good at. If you can sing, sing even if you can't hit that high note. If you can draw go further and water color, if you can sew make your own patterns. Whatever you through don't let yourself fall back into people pleasing that a big trap for self sacrificing again. I find fellowshipping is best for me and home is my sanctuary.

And if you wonderfully lucky as I am, have yourself a love story, my story would not be complete without it. The two men that came in my life that made me the vassal to bring into this world two wonderful and remarkable people, and if they had not been born, the lives of the many people they have touched, would not have been as for filling and purpose driven as they are. So in the end all it took was just one man, to make girls like me dreams come true. I always tell Rock if my father Joe Bellinger would have met you, you two would have been best of friends. Matter of fact Rock reminds me so much of my father, big, dark, strong, mans man, leader of the pack. The one you call on if you need to know who can do what and get it done kind of guy. The kind of man his sons end their phone calls with I love too dad and when his daughter says, yes daddy it just melts your heart, because whatever he just said to her, she knows can trust it. All the other times in my life I was just playing house and there was always an underbelly shadow that held a lie, but then freedom comes and you're not afraid anymore to tell someone I'm good I don't need a man to complete me, if you can't ....oh how would my son say it ...oh if you can't subscribe to my plan of what got laid out for the rest of my life then I think we just need to be friends......oh but when Mr. Rock High looked in my eyes and said, sounds like you tired of the bullshit, that's funny I'm tired too. So the journey began and what a wonderful journey it's been nothing complicated, keeping it simple. The hardest thing we worry about is how often we have to cut the grass and making sure the pipes don't freeze in the winter. We say our morning prayers and our prayers at night, we celebrate when our grandchildren are born and we have family get together when we come into a few extra dollars. We make Christmas a big deal and we always show up when we're invited and not to many times empty handed. The words I LOVE YOU is spoken at the end of every phone call and when leaving and returning. Having each other's back, front, side, harsh words are for when you think you grown, because you grown enough to apologize and explain yourself. Knowing that when you are out in the world that you represent the both of us. I truly believe that he and I knew each other in pass lives, if there is such a thing. He's not one I have to explain about the pain just because he knows, he's seen it, he's been there and we are such kindred spirits, we so welcome Freedom....

I love it when ever I hear him say

Man I wouldn't take a million dollar for her, not even all the money in the world.....

my love for you is ever lasting.............

The blessing that's over our life God the Father gave it to us freely, because He trust us to know what to do with it. You are my King and I am your Queen forever we will be R&B

The end

I woke with the morning dew

The early morning light laceed itself across my eyes
I jumped to my feet
The air was cold
The frost had not yet melt
The warm sun was on my neck
My feet touched the morning dew
I pressed down hard onto it
And my body felt a chill
I looked up at the great tree, and it's great branches embraced me
The sun wraped me in her blanket
And I cried
Mother morning asked me why I cried
I answered
I'm sorry it took so long to answer your call
The great tree branches, set me down ever so gingerly
And the ground was warm
The sun then adorned me with a gown of golden ray
And mother morning said
I just want to tell you
Let the sun shine in on them dark places that you hide in
And you will find
That God is always on your side
He will never leave you nor forsake you
Nor have you begging for love
For you are love my child
For you illuminate his love

Where ever you go
So go
And be who you are
And just like a ray
You'll go far
And with that
A breeze blew
And it was a start of a new day

Now who are you my dear
I am Barbara

fields from wince I came

Rows and rows of something so soft, and yet so hard on my grandmama back.

When she was out of my sight, how I'd run and run down those rows

Till I'd jump on her sack and there I"d take a nap

Cotton, cotton, cotton

Poems by umi
Can't sleep

What makes the night so long?

Sleep, sweet sleep

It was written in a song

And sleeps the only freedom that she knows

Untrue for me

Racing thoughts

Pictures of memories

Faces not seen or heard from in quite some time

Memories of lovers long gone

Then the thought of the future

What will become of me?

I can only pray till sleep comes and rescues me

What are you doing

What are you to do?

Are you doing what need to be done?

Are you doing what the lord ask you

  The things you are doing

Has been given you in detail and instructions were clear

        Do what you're doing

        In Jesus name

Love and it will have his approval there

 For all the world to see

What are you doing?

  You can ask me

I can't recall

Do you ever recall grandma laughter?

Her laughing out loud

I know grandma did

But not grandma

I knew of her bottom lip

When it roll back in her mouth

To let me know

She means what she say

It's just that

Her laughter escapes me

I can only recall the chuckle

And a push up

Mmmm pucker

Almost like a kiss

An act in making jokes

But a knee slapping

Belly shaking

Holla

Nope

I don't recall

Grandma laugh

Like that at all

Sunday at mothers

The tea kettle is whistling

    One at a time

Someone comes into the kitchen

They prepare toast or cereal

Washing dishes is a must

From getting up during the night

Nibbling on something throughout the night

    I got up before dawn

And sat on her bedside and cried

Just to have her hand touch my head

Fill the empty space in my head

Then her soft words

 That gave me remedy for my restlessness

Drink some tea

It did something for me

The grandchildren are leaving now

 The son picks them up and away

Another goodtime at grandmothers

Good food, hugs so tight

 Nuzzled in her bed

Laughter fills the room

 Sunday at grandma

 So much love

Printed in the United States
By Bookmasters